SPIRITUAL HEALING FOR TODAY

SPIRITUAL HEALING FOR TODAY

Raymond Charles Barker

DeVorss Publications

Spiritual Healing for Today
Copyright © 1988
by the Estate of Raymond Charles Barker

ISBN: 0-87516-607-5
Library of Congress Catalog Number: 88-70091

Second Printing, 1998

DeVorss & Company, Publisher
P.O. Box 550
Marina del Rey, CA 90294

Printed in The United States of America

CONTENTS

—

Part Three: Barkerisms—Potent Stimulants to Healing

Part Four: Treatments—Healing in Action

A WORD FROM
THE PUBLISHER

Thirteen days before Dr. Barker's passing on 26 January 1988, he and I tied up the loose ends of this, his first book in 15 years and, so unexpectedly, his last. He had had it in mind for more than a year, and I was privileged to work with him in putting it together, continuing a collaboration that had begun with the reissue of his *You Are Invisible* and that had gone forward with the *Collected Essays of Raymond Charles Barker*.

More than a decade earlier I had been fortunate enough to study under Dr. Barker in what was his last two-year course in the Science of Mind, offered at New York's First Church of Religious Science, which he had founded in 1946 at the behest of his teacher, Ernest Holmes. Upon his retirement in 1979, he moved to the California desert community of Rancho Mirage and established ties with DeVorss & Company, bringing out the first papercover edition of his very popular *Science of Successful Living*. When, a few years later, I too settled in southern California, our paths once more crossed and I had the opportunity of working with him on his books.

Spiritual Healing for Today reflects what I believe was Dr.

Barker's growing concern with the current state of the healing ministry in the New Thought movement—a concern that he pointedly voiced in his "Past President's Address" to the 71st Annual International New Thought Alliance Congress in Houston in July 1986, and one that the reader can see for himself in Dr. Barker's preface to this book. We are fortunate, I feel, to have this basic healing manual from him, and there is something unusually fitting in its being his last literary testament.

Dr. Barker's departure was sudden, as he had always wanted it to be, and it seemed almost cruelly to remove from our midst one who embodied his teaching with very great grace, a delightful wit, and incredible consistency. Richard Collins has said it for many of us: "He was absolutely true to his principles. In that regard he was as a rock. I believe that was his greatness. That and the fact that his principle was Truth."

He is deeply missed. But we have his words to us; the wonderful memory of him; and his books, which will be serving new generations when we, his "survivors," have followed him. However, we shall have some catching up to do! Looking ahead, in 1967, to his transition from this sphere of activity, he said:

I am not living just to go somewhere. I am living to go *everywhere; . . . I want to go on and on*, and I want to go on as expanded consciousness.

ARTHUR VERGARA
Editor

viii

A WORD FROM DR. BARKER

Having been in the healing ministry of the metaphysical movement in America for forty-eight years, I feel I can write on the subject of healing with authority. Having been active in the New Thought movement since 1934, I knew many of what we today call the "old-timers"—the prominent pioneers of the healing movement such as Charles Fillmore, co-founder of the Unity movement, Nona Brooks, founder of the Divine Science movement and Ernest Holmes, founder of the Religious Science movement. All of these fine teachers were devoted to spiritual healing.

This book is composed of material I have written for the *Creative Thought* magazine, published by the Religious Science International organization, with headquarters in San Diego.*

I would like to see a revival of spiritual healing based on the Divine Mind and Its clear Consciousness. I know from

*Dr. Barker's original manuscripts, however, as well as additions he later made have been used in compiling Parts I and II.—*Ed*.

experience that this system of spiritual methods is complete within itself. However, it has often been and still is diluted by other factors used in the techniques of healing. I invite you to return with me to the original methods based on Mind and on Mind alone.

January 1988   R. C. B.

PART ONE

THE FOUR OMNIS

I

OMNIPRESENCE

Whatever the Originating Cause of all there is, It must be everywhere evenly present in Its totality. In every point in space all that God is, is in full action. There is no vacuum in the divine order. All Life is active in every form of life. All Mind is active in every action of intelligence in every thinker there is. Love, the unifying action, is trying to function in every emotional situation. All of this Right Action is yours by virtue of being alive and functioning as consciousness.

Your consciousness unfolds as you realize the importance of subconsciously knowing that God is at work in every activity of your mind, body and affairs. Daily affirm in your thought and word that whatever needs to be done is being done by the Omnipresence acting in you, through you and for you. This erases all belief in stress and strain. What you seemingly can't do, this Presence and this Power can do, and does it. Relax and let the action of the Infinite Consciousness take over, and you are instantly guided to do whatever is needed to be done.

The full working of the Spirit in your thought is the way of ease and joy in living each day. Laborious living is unnecessary and futile. There is a spiritual purpose in each moment of your day. Seek it and you will find it. As a spiritual being, you cannot be frustrated, unhappy and depressed. The inner divine knowing bids you arise and become what you want to be.

There is no virtue in being unfulfilled and limited. All of God is yours when you know it and act upon the ideas revealed by your knowing. Within your thought is the fulfilling process. Its only price is your clarified and affirmative thinking. Every problem has a solution, and the way to solve it starts in your consciousness. Be still for a moment and let that idea happen in your thought which solves your problem. Mind in you as you is your eternal field of right knowing. No negative can hurt or lessen the good of anyone who practices in daily treatment the Omnipresence of the good, the true and the lovely.

All this is yours right now. There is a Light and a Way of Truth in your consciousness. You may ignore It, but It awaits your attention with loving patience.

2

OMNIPOTENCE

All Power and Intelligence is in action in your consciousness as you read this. Omnipotence always has been true, is now true and evermore shall be true. It is inevitable and inescapable. You can ignore It, but you cannot get out of It. It loads your every thought with pregnant power to accomplish. This is so whether the thought is affirmative and creative or negative and destructive.

Omnipotence is Mind's accomplishing action in all situations. The Infinite Causative Mind is not only omnipresent—meaning everywhere evenly present—but Its Omnipotence, which is all power and all possibility, is in every thought you think this day and every day of your life. You can ignore It, but It does Its work unceasingly in your consciousness. Your cooperation with It ensures your peace of mind and successful living.

Your thinking is the deciding factor in what Omnipotence produces for you. All negative emotions and thought channel all power and intelligence to create further negative states in your consciousness. Negatives beget more negatives. Affirmative thinking begets more affirmative thinking. Every moment you are deciding consciously or unconsciously the way that Divine Power produces in your affairs. The responsibility for successful living is entirely yours. Power acts through consciousness in accord with your directions.

Students of this Science cannot blame outside factors for their problems. Stop fooling yourself. Your problem is not caused by world conditions, economics or lack of anything. Problems are Power misdirected, and the result is limitation. This fact may be unpleasant but it is true. All Life responds to your consciousness by becoming that which you are thinking and believing. All good is available to every individual, but that individual has to discipline his emotions and thought to let it happen.

Select the good you want and decide that you not only can have it, but Mind will give you the ideas to get it factually in your life. Erase all doubt. Erase all fear of failure. Know that God wants you to have what you have chosen as long as it will not harm anyone else and will not harm you. Having thought through your decision, know it is already accomplished. Then relax, and Omnipotence takes over. It knows how to bring it to pass, and will bring it to pass if you will maintain an affirmative consciousness.

Omnipotence is impersonal. It knows neither good nor evil. It acts wherever thought and emotion are active in the minds of people. In your consciousness It will produce the not-good or the good as you decide Its action.

3

OMNISCIENCE

The one Mind, God, is all-knowing and is all-Science. It is everywhere evenly present filling all space and all time. It is total Idea. All creative ideas are in this Mind and they are instantly available to every man, woman and child that is now, has been and evermore shall be. Inspiration of consciousness is as available as the air you breathe. All this is a free gift to each person. The Divine Mind and Its Ideas have no awareness of human thought and its limitations. They are independent of human thought, opinions and fixed beliefs. They know not religious creeds nor so-called special people or situations. They are instantly yours when you seek them with all your consciousness.

You can know what you want to know at the instant you want to know it, once you grasp the true meaning of Omniscience. Contemplate yourself as an infinite possibility. Forget for a moment how the material world labels and measures your knowing. As consciousness you are always able to grasp the new and better ideas that now flow

7

through your thinking. These reveal the answers to all questions and the solutions to all problems. This is not too great a claim to make. The Science of Mind believes that the Allness of Spiritual Mind functions in your present flow of consciousness. This does not require intellectual exercises or intellectual attainments. God's Ideas are yours now and always will be.

Within your consciousness is Mind as Total Idea. It awaits your affirmative knowing that you have it by right of being, by right of existence. You cannot earn it, except that it does require affirmative and spiritual disciplines to know that all Mind is yours at this moment. Drawing on the Ideas of the Infinite Knower, your every need is met with ease and in order. Harmony governs the knowing consciousness, for there is no fear to disturb it and no negative speculation to cancel it. God as Omnipotence in your thought maintains you in Omniscience. You are always free to use great ideas when your mental household is in order and divinely centered on the Truth which frees you into larger and finer experiences of life, here and now.

How great is the Spiritual Inheritance which abides in fullness as our inner resources! Like all Creative Thinkers, you can draw upon Its inexhaustible inspiration and become the great individual you inwardly want to be.

4

OMNIACTION

The Divine Spirit as Infinite Mind is in total action at every point in this universe. It is the action of the All in Its domain of the All. It is spiritual energy evenly active in all time and space. Its action is only for the expanding good of all people and in all situations. It has no opposition. It is an affirmative energy and knows no negatives. It can do and does whatever needs to be done wherever it needs to be done. This is the Action of God, and this Action is omnipotent and omniscient.

All Life, Truth, Intelligence and Love are this Action. All this is instantly available to you. All It requires to be in action in your consciousness is your knowing that It is. Affirm in your own thought that this is so, because it is so for those who really believe in Truth and the wonderful results of Its Action. This is the Truth which sets you free to be all that you decide to be. It opens the gates to all that you want to be and can be as you let Omniaction into your consciousness. Its only requirement is that you know that It IS.

Knowing this perfect Action, all Mind and all Ideas are immediately available in your thinking-feeling nature. Never again need you hesitate to make right decisions. Before you need to know, the Right Idea is awaiting your need. All that God is, is within you at all times and in all places. You are the Beloved of the all-knowing Consciousness. All great unconditioned Ideas are seeking to be made manifest in the world by means of you. They have no interest in your past or your problems. They are Now Ideas and are unlimited by such terms as past, present and future. They are the action of the All, and the All is always now.

To be fully aware of Omniaction, you have to cancel out all negatives, hurts and fears. These are unnecessary millstones around your neck. Cast them off and walk free into a greater present good and a much greater future of good events and wonderful personal relationships. These can be because in the One Mind they already are. Their only price is mental discipline to daily know that only the Good can be and is yours. All Mind, Life and Love urge you to act upon this Truth.

PART TWO

HEALING:
THE FOUR OMNIS IN ACTION

I

THE SOURCE OF HEALTH AND HEALING
___

Spiritual healing is as old as man himself. It has been traced in history back to the earliest days of man's awareness. Its modern revival began around 1850 in the United States. Vital men and women experienced spiritual healing through changes in their individual consciousness. Out of this revival came two great systems of healing. One is faith healing as used in evangelical churches. Great men and women preached such healing in highly emotional atmospheres, and they had and are still having healings.

The second system is widely known as Spiritual Mind Healing or Metaphysical Healing. Its prominent teachers and ministers teach rather than preach. This type of healing is done in quiet sincerity. It has brought forth vital men and women practitioners of its method. Today there are churches and centers of spiritual mind healing throughout the world. It is a current and practical method of spiritual healing. Thousands of people everywhere can testify to the results they have had through following the instruction they have been given by teachers and the literature of this Science.

A feature of today's metaphysical healing systems is the vast quantity of literature, books and booklets available to anyone who wants to investigate its techniques and under-lying premises. Most bookshops have sections where our prominent authors' books can be purchased; and they are available in every Truth church and center. The sales of this literature are tremendous, and its readership is steadily growing. Magazines such as *Science of Mind, Creative Thought, Daily Word* and *Unity* reach great audiences of several millions of people—all of them believing in and practicing spiritual mind healing.

In all larger cities, churches and centers are located. They can easily be found by looking in the Yellow Pages of the telephone directory, listed under such headings as Religious Science, Unity, Divine Science, Christian Science and Science of Mind. People wanting information on phys-ical, mental and emotional healing should visit these church centers and study their methods. A warm welcome awaits anyone attending these churches, and qualified practitioners are always available for counseling.

The basic idea included in all systems is that the in-dividual is spiritually perfect right here and right now. There is no preaching of sin and salvation. There is a great emphasis on the need to change basic thinking from the ac-cepted negatives of the world to a true knowing that the person is perfect, spiritual and divine—that one is now, and ever shall be, perfect in body, mind and affairs. These ideas and many more will be explained in the sections that follow.

2

CAN YOU BELIEVE IT IS POSSIBLE?

In a great book it is written that "All things are possible to those who believe." This point is an essential one. Most people are certain it isn't possible, even though they may be in need of it. The first step in spiritual mind healing is to know that it is possible without reservations or doubts. God responds to affirmative thinking. It has no way of responding to negative, pessimistic and skeptical thinking.

As you study this Science and practice its affirmative thinking, you grasp the possibilities of your own consciousness. Possibilities are your spiritual birthright. They lift your thinking above the failures, the unhappiness and the illnesses of life. They are God in action in your consciousness revealing what is really so and for you can be so. You then use fewer negatives and talk fewer negatives and have fewer negatives.

You may not need physical healing, but you probably need a healing in another area of your experience, such as personal problems with people, financial difficulties and just plain frustration. All healing of any kind is possible through spiritual clear knowing of Truth and Love. The divine purpose of being is to have freedom and health in all ways and in all relationships. Spiritual ideas actually employed in consciousness do just that.

The area in your life where you are discontented is the one which needs spiritual healing, and this you can have. There is nothing casual about spiritual healing. It doesn't just happen to people who are cheery and on the surface happy. It takes place through subconscious changes, which are not easy to make—but they can be made.

Treatment, or Affirmative Prayer, will help you change your thinking over to positive, spiritual ideas. The following is a treatment, or scientific prayer, for overall well-being:

There is only one Mind, God, Infinite Good, Infinite Love, Infinite Truth. This Mind rules and governs all. This Mind is my mind now. The Life, Love and Mind of God are in action in me at this instant. I am filled completely with the Light and Spirit of Truth.

Through my mind God thinks. Through my heart God expresses Divine Love. Through my body God expresses His perfect life, health and vitality. There is no life, truth, substance or intelligence in evil; God, the Good, is all there really is, and I am surrounded and filled with It. In my life God is the only activity now taking place.

I have spiritual wisdom, spiritual perception and spiritual discernment. I love Truth, speak Truth, rejoice in Truth, for God is Truth.

So be it!

But treatment or prayer can and should be as specific as our need requires. The following is an example of treatment specifically for Divine Guidance:

God is Mind, and this perfect Intelligence is now acting in me, through me, and for me. This perfect God-Mind created me and is the thinking capacity within me. I know that in Divine Mind is the answer to every question and the fulfillment of every need. I am now definitely inspired to right action in my life by the Ideas of the Spirit which are acting in my consciousness. I know what to do, when to do it and how to do it. I am open and receptive to God's guidance, God's wisdom and God's Love. I rejoice in my sure faith in this inner wisdom, and I am successful in all my ways.

So it is!

Part Four of this book contains 34 treatments under ten comprehensive headings for your guidance and self-help.

You will find a complete discussion of Treatment/Affirmative Prayer—what it is and how to do it—in my book *Collected Essays.** You may also find it helpful to use the daily treatments that appear in such periodicals as *Science of Mind* and *Creative Thought*, or in such books as *Creative Ideas* (Holmes), *Your Needs Met* (Addington), *Special Meditations for Health, Wealth, Love and Expression* (Murphy) and *Richer Living* (Holmes/Barker). They are not to be read quickly and put aside. They should be read slowly and thoughtfully and meditated upon. They are

*Collected Essays of Raymond Charles Barker (Marina del Rey, Calif.: DeVorss & Co., 1987), from which the treatments quoted have been taken.

17

written by highly trained men and women who know and practice spiritual mind healing.

Attend your nearest Religious Science church, Science of Mind center, Divine Science church, Unity center, etc., to be with people who believe in healing and who practice it.* Look over their book department for books and pamphlets on healing. Study these until you have absorbed them, and then find more to study. If you are not near any of these centers or churches, write to the one nearest you. They will gladly send you lists of books on the subjects of health, prosperity and happiness.

Watch your beliefs, for they are causes to future experiences. What you seriously believe happens. That is the law of mental causation. We shall take a closer look at this law in the pages that follow.

*These are not the only ones. *New Thought*, a magazine published by the International New Thought Alliance (5003 E. Broadway Rd., Mesa, AZ 85206), has a directory of affiliated groups in the fifty states and overseas. *Science of Mind* and *Creative Thought* magazines list churches and centers of Religious Science.

3

THE CONSCIOUSNESS OF HEALTH

The Infinite Mind can do all things needed in your consciousness. As we saw in Part I, It is omnipotent and omniscient. It knows what to do in revealing complete health in your thought and in your emotions. This Divine Action can only be blocked by your hanging on to old negatives and symptoms. It can also be blocked by your remembrance of other peoples' illness and death. You are an independent expression of God and can be healed if you really want to be healed.

Health is a spiritual idea, and it exists in the consciousness of every person everywhere. It functions as the individual is aware of it. Being spiritual and perfect, it doesn't know what it can't do, so it is able to heal all problems in all people. It is an affirmative life-giving consciousness that heals all errors and stimulates all right thinking. It is not governed or controlled by the beliefs of the world. It is your health now and evermore shall be wherever you may be.

19

Isaiah wrote, "Arise, shine; for thy light is come, and the glory of the Lord is risen upon thee." This is your health as it is in that Mind and Heart of Being. It knows no severity of illness and no length of time in healing it. It knows you as itself and leaves you free to prove it so or to disregard it. It is constant in its spiritual work in your body when it is acknowledged by you.

Divine Health knows not the names of diseases and all other problems. Such terms are not in the divine vocabulary. There is no rhyme or reason to illnesses of any kind. They are outside the Divine Order of creative living, and to the One Mind they have no existence and certainly no reality. They appear out of one's negative thinking and false negative conclusions. They appear in order to disappear. Life knows them not, and you are always free to not know them.

Often it takes a great deal of watching your thoughts and feelings to correct them instantly. You must negate and cancel all fears of disease in any form. To invite health into your consciousness and body, you must cease from worrying. Your thinking can always be diverted to the affirmative ideas of the day. Great and good happenings are taking place, and you can note them and embody them in your thinking rather than the other, vicious, negative habits of mind. The Good awaits your perception of it. It is where you are and within your own being. It is seeking you as you are seeking it.

4

SPIRITUAL HEALING IS POSSIBLE

Sincere students of modern metaphysics have many times been healed of minor and major illnesses through applying the principles of Truth. Are the results 100% in all who use these spiritual ideas? No, but that is also true of other forms of healing. The casual reader who thinks all this is very helpful but who does not make a real effort to change his or her thinking-emotional patterns through aggressive spiritual thinking will not be helped.

You cannot successfully be an artist in any area just by playing at the methods of the selected instrument. Only a real dedication to the idea and the art chosen, followed by constant practice of the necessary techniques, will bring the ideal to pass. In spiritual mind healing the same is true. It is not a matter of hope or wishing followed by speaking well-known platitudes that creates affirmative results.

It all begins when you make a sincere decision to be normally healthy through these techniques. Unless this decision is made, there is no use in proceeding with mental tools. Other forms of healing are available, and the wisdom and experience of the medical profession are phenomenal. Outside of Christian Science, metaphysical ministers, teachers and practitioners have no rejection of medicine and its practitioners. We know that the One Mind works through these fine people.

Decision starts the spiritual process of healing. The determined consciousness then proceeds to empty all negatives out of its thinking. It defines clearly the end result of its programmed spiritual statements. It is correct self-thinking or correct self-talking in our language. This we call spiritual treatment. You deny with feeling the existence of a particular ailment and affirm with feeling your perfect health. Do this several times a day. Next, don't allow family or friends to discuss your symptoms. You don't need that return to the negative. Let all with whom you are associated know that you would enjoy pleasant conversation about other things than your problem. We will consider spiritual treatment in more detail a bit later.

Know that the total Mind and Heart of God are supporting your clear statements of Truth. Everything is for you. There is nothing against you. You are only clearing your consciousness and affirming what you really are. All the healing processes of life itself are responding to your declared word. The expulsion of negative feeling sets free the life power in you to do its perfect work.

All things are possible to the individual who has decided to demonstrate greater health through spiritual means. All that God is responds to the knowing mind and the loving heart.

5

SUBCONSCIOUS CAUSATION

All creation, including the individual, is the result of ideas in Mind. What God creates lives forever. What man interferes with ends in a negative. Your subconscious mind is the creative consciousness of all that you are and all that you will ever be. Begin today and watch the workings of this great emotional field in your consciousness. It is spiritual and omnipotent when it is used correctly to maintain your health of mind and, in turn, the health of every phase of your life.

That is its right use. Now we shall think of its incorrect use. Here is where fears and worries will dominate your daily thought unless they are curtailed by you. You can always change your thinking. In the subconscious are your expectations regarding health and disease, life and death, love and hate. Without realizing what you were doing emotionally from your date of birth to this day, experiences, negative people and hurts have registered and been given emotional power. These negatives and many more seek to control your conscious thinking. Correct spiritual treatment will diminish them, provided you are sincere in doing your spiritual knowing each day.

All illness and disease are the physical appearances of serious subconscious negative patterns of thought which have been operating in your consciousness for a long, long time. Illness doesn't just happen on a certain calendar date. It has been brewing in your subconscious over an extended period. When it happens, you need to know that the healing action of God is at the point where the problem is.

You are never apart from the healing process of the Spirit of perfect life and health. You are a beloved individual and are a vital part of the creative process of life. However, the wise student of this Science quietly contemplates the possible cause of his problem. Knowing that the cause is in his or her subconscious, this person starts the healing process by thinking of God, thinking of health, strength and vitality. Do whatever the medical doctor tells you to do, but be sincere in your thinking of God and health. Your healthy mental attitude and expectation of complete recovery is the greatest cooperative element you can contribute to the efforts of the medical profession.

Ernest Holmes, who formulated the Science of Mind, has written that the thing that makes you sick is the thing that makes you well. Both are subconscious mental and emotional processes, and you can direct them by your clear knowing that you are spiritually perfect no matter what the opinion or outward appearance may be. This knowledge understood is the finest spiritual insurance policy for your health there is. The only cost is not money but sincere spiritual thinking for a few moments each day.

6

THE EXPECTANT CONSCIOUSNESS

Unless you expect to be healed, there is no possibility of healing. There is a Divine Expectancy in this method of healing. Your whole consciousness needs to be turned around from its negatives to the side of affirmative knowing that the healing is not only possible, but at this very instant is taking place. Declare aloud, "I am now free of all doubt." Divine Right Action is then free to operate because all the negatives have ceased their dominion in thought and have become as nothing.

The most important factor in spiritual healing is the personal factor. Unless you know, not merely believe or hope, that the Infinite knows you as Itself and therefore as perfect health and well-being, your faith is not sufficient for your demonstration. Your consciousness is a center in the perfect knowing consciousness of God. When it is free of all erroneous thinking, including fear, your health can spring forth speedily. Daily spiritual treatment is vital to the healing process. It provides the mental and emotional atmosphere in which the good can happen.

The Divine cannot act through negatives. It does act through positive and affirmative clearance of consciousness. This is the work you have to do, and it is not casual; it is real mental work hour after hour and day after day. It is demanding and often boring, but it has to be done. Take time out for refreshing breaks by reading Truth literature and speculating on the good things you will be doing in the future. Never place a time limit on the healing. That is dictating to the spiritual intelligence that does its perfect work when it is not impeded by your questions and false beliefs.

While you are doing your correct mental work on spiritual ideas, all Life and all Intelligence are responding to you. All this is in action in every cell of your body doing its perfect restorative work. You are always in the Divine Presence and known in the Divine Mind. You and your health are one. All Life is living in you at this instant of time.

Now you expect to be healthy, vital and free of all physical limitations. This is happening because your consciousness is able to let it happen by knowing the Truth—that you are spiritual and divine. This is so, and your right thinking makes it so. The Truth fully known is the Truth fully demonstrated. By means of you, this is taking place. Now in your consciousness is the glory of health and the joy of living fully and richly. For this you rejoice, give thanks and are glad.

7

HEALING IS OFTEN UNCOMFORTABLE

In order to be healed through spiritual methods you may find it uncomfortable to have to give up some of your choicest old negative beliefs. Do you honestly feel worthy of a spiritual change in your consciousness? The sense of unworthiness is a metaphysical sin. It blocks many doors through which new ideas are trying to come into your awareness. You must be clear that as a spiritual creation you are worthy of being free of the illness, the problem or whatever it is that is restricting you. In your own consciousness, state that you are worthy of all that God is and that you are worthy of perfect health right now.

Search your memory for old hates and present hates. They prevent your consciousness from affirmative action. Cease justifying your pet hates, hurts and other false ideas of the past and present. Remember that in this system of spiritual thought the universe has no place for self-martyrdom. Such people cannot be healed by the action of Truth. You are only the victim of your own thought. No

27

other individual's thoughts can affect you unless you invite them into your consciousness and believe their false claims. Then they operate negatively in your thought through your permission.

Another idea which needs to be considered by those seeking spiritual healing is: will you be uncomfortable without your pet peeves, your self-justifications, and your certainty that other people prevent you from being your real self? All this has to be healed in consciousness before there can be a healing in body, mind or affairs. Spiritual mind treatment, which is scientific prayer applied with sincerity, will erase these from your subconscious thought patterns. It is written that we should not have any other gods than the one true God. Our deeply accepted negative ideas are false gods. Their elimination is possible through a definite study of the Science of Mind and related teachings. You set yourself free when you know the Truth which you really are.

All the above ideas may seem too much to correct. If you have a trained spiritual practitioner, you can talk all of this out. Don't expect your loved ones and your close friends to understand the inner changes you are making. A trained practitioner offers you no personal opinions, never sits in judgment, and suggests methods of spiritual treatment that will help you to self-see what needs to be cleared in your consciousness.

At the moment, all this may seem complicated; but it is necessary. Gradually the light breaks through in your thought and you are truly free. This is the Light which lighteth every person who seeks Truth and loves Truth.

8

DO YOU REALLY KNOW GOD?

—

There is only one God, one Mind and one Love. Each person has his or her own concepts, beliefs and a little understanding of this creative Spirit. Ask yourself how well you really know God. If you want a spiritual healing of a physical difficulty, you had better know what God or Cause is and how It works. A surface awareness of the creative power is good while attending church services, but it will never heal even a mild cold. You need serious, quiet thinking about the nature of Life within you, as you. Don't just repeat theological terms. They are out of date and won't heal a thing. Use your everyday vocabulary to at least partially define God, health and your own consciousness. Be natural. Be yourself.

There is a wonderful simplicity to the Divine process of Being. Complicated and theoretical thinking never awakens this inner resource. Calm down; quiet down and think of what Life is doing in your mind and body at this instant. It reveals Its healing power in quietness. The Life which created your body and the Mind which created your consciousness are one process, not two. These are now totally active in you as you. But they need your conscious awareness in order to come to the surface. Quietly state to your own subconscious mind that health is a Divine gift to you. Now affirm its perfect action in your consciousness and in your body. Do this a few minutes at a time. As you do this, keep expanding your spiritual awareness by using more and different terms to explain to yourself what God and the healing power really is.

Do not make hard work of this treating. The minute it seems to be hard work is the moment to stop. Paul wrote to not be weary in well doing. Now is the time to state in your consciousness that you are health and not sickness— that all the mental and emotional subconscious causation of disease is a lie and the father of lies. State that all such negative causation is now erased from your consciousness and that you are health. Use the word *health* and not the word *healed*. The word *healed* denotes a process. The word *health* is a total now fact. Dwell on this, and absorb its meaning.

Always there arises the question of how long it will take before the healing actually takes place. The very question prevents the healing. Healing happens when the awareness of the allness of God takes place in your consciousness. When you can no longer conceive of yourself as the illness, God's Mind takes over your consciousness, and the healing is instantaneous. Remember the adage that practice makes perfect. This is a truth of spiritual treatment.

9

DO YOU REALLY KNOW YOURSELF?

Very few people really know themselves. Rarely do they seek the inner world of consciousness. They are so busy with outer goals that they have no time for self-exploration and self-meditation. In this teaching, the inner world of mind and emotions is primary, and the outer world of experience is always secondary. What you do is not as important as knowing why you do it. All causation of your acts, your failures and your successes is in consciousness, your awareness of yourself. True spiritual instruction leads you to study what you are in order to understand who you are.

All spiritual healing is an inner process of changing your convictions from belief in illness to correct knowing of God as your health. This is why a daily reading of Truth literature and your daily spoken spiritual treatment affirming your perfect health are important. Spiritual healing is never casual. It is a serious business of changing beliefs, attitudes and expectancies. Think often of the nature of God as Mind, Love, Truth, Health, etc. Such thinking keeps your attention on the pure cause of healing. It does not deal with side effects. It takes you to the inner center of your consciousness and maintains you in an affirmative attitude so that the action of God as your health can take place.

The body cannot create disease in any form. Your body is an effect acted upon at every instant by the thinking-feeling nature of your consciousness. Matter cannot make itself sick. Only mind can create negatives which are then acted out through the body. This is why it is so important to know yourself as consciousness. Spiritual healing takes place in consciousness first and in the body second. Your medical doctor and his help will assist your body in the healing process, and this is good. But the final act of healing is in your knowledge of yourself as God in action.

Repetition of a spiritual idea or belief will always cause eventual subconscious acceptance. This is our form of prayer, and we call it scientific prayer. We are not trying to change the Deity. We are using techniques that align our consciousness with the Divine Consciousness, which knows only health. Repeat daily to yourself that you are spiritual, perfect and divine. Talk to yourself about your oneness with the Divine Cause. It will seem strange at first, but soon you will feel at home with the metaphysical method of healing all varieties of problems.

All power is centered in your consciousness. It is impersonal. It does not sit in judgment and does not condemn. It is yours to direct. This is the spiritual power that heals. It is yours by right of being. As you use it correctly, it glorifies the God that you are.

10

GOD UNLIMITED

The key to all spiritual healing of body problems is a change of belief and deep affirmative knowing in consciousness. There is no mystery to spiritual mind healing. It works for anyone who applies its simple techniques. Pure and perfect Mind does not know your age, your religious beliefs, your errors or your virtues. It only knows you as Its beloved action of consciousness. It responds to your thought and acts upon it. It is not owned by any one religious system. It is available to all who want Its healing balm.

God as unlimited and unconditioned Mind can do the impossible and the unexpected. It does not know that one illness is difficult to heal and another is easy to heal. It has no gradations and is not under any law of comparisons. Its healing, perfecting activity is in every individual's consciousness. But It can only move into action when there is an awareness of It and a desire on your part to be healed. Where there is no belief in It, It cannot heal. When you decide to be healed by the action of Truth, there is an immediate response of fresh life, health and healing.

God responds to your receptivity and your new expectancy. It knows what to do, how to do it and does it, provided It has your complete cooperation in right and affirmative knowing. In your thought and speech deny any and all doubts as to Its ability, power and presence. It is always where you are. This divine action doesn't know your problem. It only knows you as perfect expression of Its total Being. This is the healing activity.

The full cooperation of the person seeking to be healed by spiritual therapy is essential to the healing process. Half-hearted cooperation will not bring about any positive results. Many people who turn to spiritual mind healing are enthusiastic and cooperative for a few days. Then their expectancy wavers and other interests absorb their mental attention. Later they tell others that spiritual healing didn't work. It didn't work because they didn't follow through to the full demonstration. Usually from the beginning they didn't really believe it would heal them.

God requires your whole consciousness to heal you. No wonder the great spiritual teachers have said, "O ye of little faith." It is easy to say yes to a spiritual program, but it is a very different thing to give it one hundred percent of your thought and feeling. Fortunately, there are the few who do practice spiritual mind healing and have excellent results. Such ones have proven its availability and its Truth.

11

UNCHANGING GOD IS
UNCHANGING HEALTH

––––

There is only one thing to be healed and that is the consciousness of the individual having the illness. The Infinite Spirit does not have any awareness of illnesses or ailments. Its consciousness is aware of the health, the vitality and the perfection of each of its beloved creations. It knows you as Itself. It knows you as Its action of great ideas. It has no comprehension of anything unlike Itself. Its awareness is of total perfection in and through Its entire creation.

"All is Infinite Mind and its infinite manifestation." A great teacher—Mary Baker Eddy—stated this, and it is the Truth of every individual. The physical body and all your seeming difficulties are temporary effects of not knowing the true Divine Cause. God, the perfect knower, has healed thousands throughout history and is equally active right now in the correct knowing of those who truly seek and find that Health which has never been sick or limited in any way. Unchanging God is unchanging Health.

To seek and find health requires full cooperation of your consciousness. To think and sense spiritual health for five minutes and then begin to waver in your attention will not heal anything. If your attention wavers, pick up a magazine, booklet or book of metaphysics and concentrate on its contents. This will sustain the healing consciousness. Many ask if there aren't physical things which they should do to help the healing. The answer is no. Spiritual healing is independent of physical methods. A great teacher of this Truth living in England often told his students, "Do what your medical doctor tells you to do, but keep on treating and knowing the Truth while you are doing it." I agree with this statement. God must be primary in your thought under all conditions to let the healing action take place.

Never close out your possible good. Your healing through spiritual mind treatment may come through many channels. You will intuitively know what to do and who can assist you in clearing your consciousness of all belief in illness. Condemn no method or system that can help you, be it medical or metaphysical. God is in action in all ways of healing and helping. But your consciousness is the true healing agency. First God and then man. All is the Truth in action when you truly know it.

Spiritual healing is serious business for the person who employs the Divine process. But never lose your sense of humor. To be able to laugh at a negative is to free yourself from that negative. Divine Love responds to the happy and peaceful consciousness and speeds up the healing process.

12

KEY IDEAS IN SPIRITUAL HEALING

There is a law of Mind which is a law of belief. What you believe with your full thought and feeling will happen in your experience. Note that it requires your full thought and accompanying feeling to accomplish the belief. This takes thought dedicated to the premise of Perfect God, Perfect Individual and Perfect Being. This is the metaphysical basis of all spiritual healing. To have results you must discard all beliefs of unworthiness and all beliefs in the devil, hell and predestination. Such beliefs prevent the action of God from healing the believer.

Solve your own problems before you try to help others. You cannot heal others while you need healing. You are not the saviour of other people. These methods of healing can be used by both sinner and saint. Both terms are relative. The Divine Mind does not know such classifications. It only knows you as a spiritual offspring of Itself. Stop trying to convince God that you are sick. That is a waste of thought and emotion. Be still in your consciousness and know that perfect life is yours right now. It is a free gift of the Spirit.

Are you good enough for Infinite Mind to heal you? The answer is that the Truth knows no measurements of goodness. It doesn't know evil in any form and It has no condemnation of any individual. Stop all negative speculation and begin to think as God thinks. This releases all worry and strain. Also cease all condemnation of other people. Mind your own business and stop making false judgments. In your consciousness you are the one to be healed, and this takes some spiritual understanding on your part.

Don't wait until you are really ill to start thinking of your health as spiritual. When you are aware of the first symptom of an illness, that is the instant to begin spiritual treatment. Set aside time each day for metaphysical reading. Follow this with audible statements that only health can exist in your body. Clear your consciousness with audible statements of Truth. Do this with sincerity and make every effort to actually believe what you are saying. God always responds to such mental work.

Finally, search within yourself for the probable emotional cause. Nothing makes you sick but your own negative beliefs, hurts and disappointments. Face your negative mental states and be frank with yourself about them. You need not tell others, but you do need self-examination to find the causes of what is now appearing in your body as illness. Remember that the God Presence within you is the source and continuity of your health. Perfect life in your mind and body responds to your knowing the Truth which heals.

PART THREE

BARKERISMS:
POTENT STIMULANTS TO HEALING

I

GOD AND MAN

Back of all circumstances is a Divine Constant, that which is eternal, true and unchanging, that which is God.

God as a theological argument leads you into, and keeps you in, the wilderness. But God as a present action, right where you are, takes you where you want to go.

The nature of God is Absolute. But as we experience It, It seems to be relative.

41

We must have a deep-seated conviction that *all* is an out-picturing of God.

Everything is the action of God, taking place *in* God for the glory of God.

"I AM"—the name of God—is of the present, not the future or the past—not "will be" or "was."

God is always knowing Himself to be. What God knows Himself to be causes us to be. We are the action of His knowing.

Man is God made visible. Man is the visibility of the Creative Power. Man is the representative of God at this level of consciousness.

There is not God's Life and your life. There is only one Life—God's.

Man is a necessary complement of God. Without man, God has no way to distribute His ideas.

All of God is at every point of God and available at every point of God. This being so, God is everywhere. And everything that God is, is at every point in the everywhere.

In Infinite Mind, every person exists as a separate entity, but not as a *separated* entity.

The universe displays the law and order of God. Man displays the intuition of God.

What God conceives, man reveals.

You are consciousness in Mind, knowing yourself as form.

We are a temporary form in a permanent Principle.

All of God is where I am and in me, but It is also everywhere else.

The Power in which we are has all the greatness we can ever be.

The thing I am was fulfilled before creation began.

Only that in me which is God can feed me at all levels.

44

God is unlimited. Man is self-limited.

God is Wisdom and we should claim it.

God never specialized anyone—but anyone can specialize God. God was the specialty of Jesus.

Whatever you define God to be is your definition of yourself.

Whatever you attach to "I am," that you become.

You are an evolving person. You have come out of all time and are going *to* all time, from glory to glory, led by the image of the Lord. There is a perfect image at the center to cause what you are.

Individuality means self-choice, complete freedom, Spirit personified.

We are giving and receiving stations of Mind-action.

In this teaching, we look upon the individual not as body, but as a sum total of mind action through the years.

We are living, walking, talking, loving expressions of God.

You, as you, are not limited to the point where you are, although you appear to be.

When we say "God is Love," we mean the love we are now using on anything we love in our world.

What I believe about God doesn't do me much good if I am sick, in debt and cannot get along with people. I must make my belief work.

You are an idea in Mind. God is eternally improving His idea of you, for He never runs out of new concepts of Himself.

There is that in you—Spirit—which is unconditioned regardless of what you have done to condition yourself.

When you can talk about God as easily as you can talk about bacon and eggs or the weather, then you know God.

You are important to God and to man. But first, you have to be important to yourself.

If you were good enough for the Creative Power to create, you ought to be good enough for yourself.

Your highest thought of God will always find a spiritual response.

A great test is to see God in the commonplace.

We are one with everyone else on the face of the globe—at the subconscious level. We are a separate action of God only at the conscious-mind level. We are one with all Life.

You will never see God unless you can look into the face of your neighbor and see It there. No man will ever see his conception of God because God is not a conception. God is the Reality.

48

We do not tell God how to run His business. We get ourselves out of the way so God's business can work in us.

I now open my mind to the God of this instant, the Infinite Spirit of this hour, the great creative ideas of this moment. I weep not over the past. I rejoice in the God of the NOW.

2

MIND AND CONSCIOUSNESS

The world is a panorama of an operative Mind.

We live in a universe of intelligence which always expresses the Mind of God. Our thinking determines our experience. Our mood sets the pattern and the Law of Mind produces our subconscious desires. We are always established in the results of our own creations.

The universal Principle of Life is that of a creative Mind, a creative Intelligence, which acts through your mind producing around you what is *in* your mind.

51

You are a thinker, and what you think is thought into a Law, which acts upon it in exact correspondence to what you thought.

Thought is creative because God is the thought *and* the Creator.

Mind is divine in nature, spiritual in origin and perfect in operation.

The point of control is at the level of mind.

A controlled mind with an essential goodness at the center can handle any problem.

What man can think, man can do.

Our mental atmosphere is the result of all we have said, done or thought, consciously or subconsciously perceived.

Everyone is where he is by right of consciousness, and when he is through with where he is, his consciousness moves him to his next right place.

Your mind is your world because your mind is the action of the Creative Power.

Every time you use your mind and emotions at their highest peak, at their greatest level and in their grandest way, you are doing what the Infinite has always been doing.

We are here to do a great work because the Mind that created us knew what It wanted us to do when It created us.

Every time we think, we set the Mind of God in action.

It must happen *in* us before it can happen *to* us.

Your consciousness is the center and circumference of your experience.

Your present state of consciousness will continue your present experience.

An expanded experience will never happen until an expanded consciousness precedes it.

Your only enemy is yourself, and the only thing that can hold you back is your own mind.

Your mind determines your experience. Your thinking and emotions determine what you are. What you are determines what you have; and what you have is nothing but the outer indication of what you are.

Your consciousness is organized to action, not to inaction. Anything that tends to reduce the action of consciousness is not a healthy thing.

God can only act according to your current thought, not the hopes you had ten years ago.

We demonstrate our present state of consciousness—not what we wish we were.

You can only see around you what exists within you. Viewpoint is a state of consciousness.

Consciousness extends around and through the body. Anything you think, you think all over you.

Your present consciousness at its best and expanded is your vision.

Ideas are the key to everything. The efficiency of your mind is determined by the ideas which operate it.

An idea unfolds according to Law. A plant in the window-box does not fight the earth, the sun, the rain. It uses them. When we use the ideas of God, our consciousness unfolds according to Law.

If we use willpower in trying to gain a much-wanted thing, we push it away.

Imagination is one of the great powers of the mind. It gives form and outline to mood, the mold which determines the form. Imagination must be controlled if we are disciplined students of Truth.

Only original thinking is productive in your experience—not competitive thinking, not comparison thinking, but original thinking.

The moment that consciousness no longer has any fields to conquer, it begins to decay.

When the human mind thinks "Why should I try something new and different?" the routine becomes the rut, and the rut becomes the grave.

The moment you take something for granted, a point of dissolution appears, for you cannot take life for granted. There is nothing in the universe that seeks to maintain the old except the human mind.

Right thinking about yourself will automatically move you into your right place.

My consciousness is the force I place in the world.

Sympathy is the lowering of the mind to the problems of another person.

A truly great person is only great to the extent that he lets an idea flow through him which enriches the universe.

You and I, as consciousness, should choose what we want to do or be. Then all the power of Spirit moves toward its demonstration.

Where the attention is, the desire follows. And where the desire follows, the emotions back up the original purpose.

The direction of your language indicates the direction of your thinking.

Thinking must be straight and affirmative, not foggy. The universe does not decide what you want. You will always get the average until you select the best. "For by thy words thou shalt be justified and by thy words thou shalt be condemned" (Matthew 12:37).

We don't call on the name of Edison to turn on the light. We do not call on the name of God to turn on power. We only need to recognize *It* and know *It* is there.

You are the only thinker, distributor and employer of your mind.

We can do anything we wish if we will stop scattering our energy and organize our thinking, if we will live with wisdom. *Think* of what you want, *talk* in terms of what you want, *expect* what you want and *act as though you had it.*

Many people want things at the conscious level but not at the subconscious level. The block in demonstration may be this. Make definite denials of this block.

To have a real faith is to be so convinced of something that we accept it in the subconscious.

We are *here* consciously. We are *everywhere* subconsciously.

The subconscious mind is an individual function in a universal field of action.

Every thought you have ever thought moves to the subconscious and thinks on eternally.

Your subconscious mind is about ninety-eight per cent of you. Bless it and use it wisely.

Watch your mind and keep it out of the cesspool of human opinions.

Trouble doesn't start in the world. It starts first in the mind before it appears in the world. A mental state always precedes action.

Steadfast awareness of Spirit in man will minimize his major troubles and keep them at an emotional minimum.

Every time we work with a fear, every time we work with a worry or a doubt, we are taking the most ingenious mechanism that Creation ever produced—the mind— and using it wrongly.

61

Watch consciousness as you would watch dynamite in the hands of a child. When an obstruction arises, treat and treat and treat.

The sum total of the consciousness that we are is what we are looking through and looking at. For we see only ourselves in our world. When we see trouble, it means we must get clear in our own consciousness.

If I know I am in an originating Power, then I contemplate It and let It do it. The Power of the universe can and does get me out of trouble.

The Infinite Something that fashioned man out of Itself is always working for the good of Its own creation. It never allows the destructive forces of the human mind to win out in the long run.

3

GOOD AND EVIL,
POSITIVES AND NEGATIVES

Goodness in the midst of evil is infectious. It is as a light in the darkness.

We can destroy evil but we can't create good, because it always was. We can destroy disease but we cannot create health, because it always was.

Fighting evil on a material basis never clears it. It only moves it.

Evil appears to disappear.

Evil destroyed is good appearing.

There is no such thing as an evil person, but only a person using life tragically. When we condemn or hate such a person, we only deliver more evil power into their hands.

The perception of a negative becomes the acceptance of the negative. And, the acceptance of the negative becomes the defeat of the individual.

When you arrive at the decision that any negative in your world can be destroyed, and that you are going to destroy it, then your mind, as a spiritual function, moves in a positive way upon it, dissolves it, nullifies it and erases it out of your experience.

There is no permanent evil, there is no permanent negation—because consciousness by its own nature will eventually improve.

Negatives are ignorance; affirmatives are wisdom.

You can mourn a negative as long as you choose, but the universe never mourns a negative. It is too busy producing a positive.

A positive is eternal. A negative is a temporary cover-up.

Faith, hope and love are the positive involvements of our world. Fear and worry are the negative involvements.

When you get clear on a positive, you will have the positive as long as you stay clear.

Obvious negatives are easy to handle. It's the subtle ones that come trickling in at the back door of your mind that you have to watch.

Every negative idea is vicious, no matter how small it seems to you. Think anything as long as it is a creative, joyous, free experience.

With a spiritual technique, consistently applied, you can minimize any negative emotion to a point of absolute unimportance.

Having an unwavering faith in the Invisible causes the mass of negatives to be reduced in power.

When we cross out our negatives and let them die, everything separating us from God is removed.

The only blasphemy there is, is the misuse of Mind for negative speculation.

Casual negative thinking does not cause serious sickness. A negative, repeated until it is subconscious, causes serious sickness.

Watch your minor negatives and you will always control your major ones.

A positive person declaring positive principles produces positive results.

A positive announced does something. But it can do nothing unless you accept yourself as positive.

"No" is the disintegrating action. "Yes" is the integrating action.

We should always be saying "yes" to a yes. Too often, we affirm our negatives.

You are the receiver of negation only to dissipate it.

Worry is the enveloping of a problem idea with a negative emotional atmosphere which clouds our true vision of the idea.

Bondage appears to disappear. Any negative on your pathway is there only as long as you maintain the negative.

Fear is a universal negation. The statement "I have no fear" is a spiritual truth, not necessarily a material one. We have to say it. By saying it, we set up a new cause in order to set up a new effect.

Sin is the misdirection of thought which causes a negative to appear. A ten-minute period of deep fear is as great a sin as any breaking of the moral code.

Be diplomatic but don't lie. You can always find something affirmative to say about any person or situation.

4

SICKNESS, HEALTH
AND HEALING

———

"I am one with all the wisdom, all the mind, and all the health there is. I and the Father are one. I am Spirit." The moment you become ill, it is because you have forgotten these truths about yourself.

Sickness is always a temporary acceptance of an unnecessary negative state of mind.

Disease is an impersonal thought force that operates through people but does not belong to them.

71

A sickness is a finished thing. Something is trying to get out of the body.

There is a health in man that is greater than what he does with his body.

Sickness is the dying out of evil so that health can appear.

Failure of emotional expression results in illness.

Illness is energy mobilized for action but not used creatively.

We cannot afford to linger in morbidity unless we want to linger in disease.

The healing of sickness must embody spiritual growth or the sickness will return.

Psychologists discovered that the intellect couldn't cure, but that desire could.

Jesus healed the man who was "sick of the palsy" (Matthew 8:6). When you are sick of being sick, you will get well.

All spiritual healing, in the last analysis, is nothing but spiritual self-perception.

When we find out what's wrong with a person, we rarely find out what's right with him.

A correct understanding of the nature of God and of your relationship to Him will help you to cure yourself, because it will make you realize that when you recognize yourself as Life, you are not invoking a power. You are directing a Power.

Healing action can only take place at a point where there is agreement with it. At that instant, you are it.

Spiritual Mind healing is not done by man, but by God. It is done by the introduction into the human mind of a factor not hitherto active.

A practitioner destroys a negative illusion. A practitioner lifts the veil and lets God shine through.

Healing shrines do a wonderful work at the emotional level. But it is not necessary to have a place set apart, of beautiful pageantry. Our thought is the real agency.

5

PRAYER AND TREATMENT

Every religion has taught a different language of prayer and every religion has had results from prayer. The purpose of prayer is to establish a creative mood.

Prayer is a conscious mind technique.

I am always praying as long as I am thinking. Not the little me but the Divine I.

75

The response to prayer comes out of the creative mood which is established by the prayer, and not by the words.

There is nothing to ask; there is only something to know.

Prayer is a field that can always be explored. It is only limited by our concept of it.

If you cannot pray on a busy street or in your home, you cannot pray on a mountain or in a cathedral.

A treatment is Love directed by Mind. A treatment is your feeling nature, directed by your knowing nature.

When you give a treatment, you are Love being directed by God's Mind for a creative purpose.

Treatment doesn't cure. The change of consciousness, as a result of treatment, cures.

Treatment is self-clearance, the elimination of obstructions that have kept the positives from working.

Every treatment does something at the subconscious level. No treatment is ever lost.

Every treatment registers everywhere.

Treatment begins and ends in the thought of the one giving the treatment. When it is finished in one place (the mind), it is finished everywhere.

When we give a treatment, we are thinking. We are meeting, opposing, neutralizing, erasing fear, failure, sense of loss and other negatives.

Every treatment should contain a statement against fear.

Each time our thought hits fairly and squarely, it erases just as surely and as definitely as one would erase a chalk line.

A denial removes the tarnish from your old ideas. It is the erasive quality of treatment.

Treatment takes away the negatives to reveal the positives that were always there.

A treatment cannot eliminate a negative without replacing it with a positive.

Every treatment is communion, unifying us with the expanded area of God-consciousness.

The more terms for God we use in treatment, the more effective the treatment will be. We cannot heal without using the term *God* or its equivalent.

A pure treatment is a statement of yourself as God in some aspect.

A treatment is a therapy because it is "I" beginning to understand myself.

Dare to affirm "I AM." Then that which you are will move out into your world.

Every treatment is a warrior going against a problem to destroy it.

Treatment must always have a specific end in view.

Treatment for health causes the Law to eliminate disease. Treatment for prosperity causes the Law to eliminate lack.

The time to treat for health is when you are healthy. The time to treat for love is when you are loving and being loved. The time to treat for peace of mind is when you are happy. Then you can give the treatments in the mood and tone of their own atmosphere.

Set up the atmosphere of love, then treat the condition.

We know words of themselves do not heal. It is the feeling that flows through the words that heals.

Use any sentence and put a spiritual quality in it. This is therapy.

The instant you open your mouth in treatment, you are the mouthpiece of God.

Mind knows. Mind speaks. The patient, being in the same Mind, accepts.

We do not heal a patient in treatment. We get rid of evil.

81

Medicine treats disease. We treat mental causation.

My job is to give the treatment. It is God's job to execute it.

Results cannot be judged by the personality of the practitioner.

"Amen" stops your responsibility in treating.

In treatment, we can step outside of time and short-circuit criticism, limitation and lack. Treat *back*. God recognizes no time.

Power only knows and operates in the NOW. "Now is the accepted time" (2 Cor. 6:2).

When we need a boost, we should get it via treatment. We have the machinery for it.

We should take time every morning to do our daily specific mental work. It is the only way there is to maintain a control over the floodgates of the universal subconscious mind so that negatives cannot enter.

We are Life and we have no adversary. There is no power in the world to prevent our demonstration.

PART FOUR

TREATMENTS:
HEALING IN ACTION

I

BASICS

———

I KNOW MY SOURCE

I am not self-created. I am a living result of a dynamic Consciousness which created me out of Itself. All Mind and all Love are my source and continuity. I am consciousness aware of my own reality. I am cause to my world of effects. This is the Truth of all I am and all I ever shall be. Knowing this, I am secure in my daily living.

In my consciousness, which is based on spiritual knowing, I have no fear, anxiety or worry. I think what I want and want what I think. I have total authority over the affairs of my individual world by right of correct knowing of Truth. My consciousness is now clear of all negative emotions. I am free to be the creating individual which I am. I bring to pass my programmed good without struggle or strain. God in me as me is great.

I draw upon my inner spiritual resources of love and peace. These maintain my consciousness in balance. I set myself free of personality problems. Never again shall I be hurt or depreciated by loved ones, business associates and friends. I am that I AM which perfect God is. I know my source, and I bear witness to this knowing.

I KNOW THAT MIND IS ALL IN ALL

Pure God-Consciousness is all there really is. It is omnipresent, omnipotent and omniscient. There is no place where Mind is not. I am consciousness functioning in the Larger and Perfect Knowing. All that I am is spiritual and divine. I am an eternal action in the universal Mind. My thinking this day affirms this Truth which I truly am. With wisdom and love, I prove these statements to be true. I am the evidence of Pure Being made manifest.

Right ideas are my birthright. They reveal themselves in my consciousness and give of themselves to my consciousness. They alert me to the right ways of living in the here and now. Spiritual ideas are the basis of my health, my prosperity, avenues to give and receive love, and my ability for complete self-expression. They are the premise of all my thinking and feeling. I think and know God's Ideas easily.

I know spiritual truth, and I am not receptive to the negatives of the world or of other people. I reject them and all the troubles which accompany them. Life, love and wholesomeness are mine, and I appreciate their action in my consciousness. They bring to me the right people and the right situations. I live in peace, in joy and in fulfillment. All is good.

2

MIND IN ACTION
___

INTELLIGENCE GOVERNS MY THINKING

The total and complete Divine Consciousness created me out of Itself. I am a spiritual knower in a mental law that responds to my knowing. I am intelligence and all my thinking today is intelligent thinking. Therefore, there is no place in my consciousness for negatives in any form. I am mentally and emotionally free to create the good which I want, and I do this right now. I know the fullness of life, love and prosperity. I accept them as my own.

Every problem that will appear today I meet instantly with right thinking. This awakens a spiritual idea in my consciousness for the solution of the difficulty. I have no fear of problems. I solve them at once as they appear in my experience. My thinking is based on God, the one perfect originating Mind. My thinking proves that spiritual ideas can meet every need as and when required. In my consciousness are all the spiritual ideas I need for every day.

I appreciate my consciousness, for it is the cause of all that I want for richer living. It is the source of all my true happiness and love. My intelligent use of mind not only solves my difficulties but it maintains me in a creative consciousness that is wonderful. I rejoice that I have this teaching of spiritual thinking.

MY QUIET THINKING REVEALS TRUTH

God, the living Truth, is always at peace within Itself. Now I still the anxieties of my hurried thinking in order that my consciousness will know the living Truth of my good at this moment. I know that my life is centered in good, in order and in peace. I rest from my usual concerns and let the eternal peace abide in fullness in my thinking. In the quiet of my mind great spiritual ideas are revealed. I accept them and follow through on them.

It is good to relax from all fear, worry and doubt. This calm peace is a healing power that sets my consciousness free to create the good, the true and the right. This is now taking place in all my relationships, my business affairs and my health and well-being. Right Action prevails in my life today. This Right Action in my life is always loving, kind and peaceful.

All the good there is now responds to my quiet affirmative knowing. Whatever in my life needs to be done for my more effective living is done now by the Mind and Heart of God. I let this take place, for all negative interference in my thought is dissolved. I am a new person in a new experience governed by right ideas, and I know I am on the right pathway.

I WELCOME NEW IDEAS

The starting point of all things is mental causation. It is Infinite Mind creating out of Itself by means of new ideas. My consciousness is one with the Universal Consciousness and Its ideas. Out of these ideas come new, greater forms of good. They improve my present situations and reveal wonderful happenings today. They are now creating by means of my consciousness, enriching my life with new experiences, friends and unfoldment.

I enjoy changes taking place in my life due to these spiritual ideas invigorating my thought. All passivity and lack of interest leave my subconscious mind. I am alert to the new, fresh and different. These cause me to grow in wisdom and pleasure. They open my eyes to the glory of fine living available to me as a spiritual thinker. These ideas expand my good and lessen my negatives. They maintain me in ease, order and prosperity.

Watching ideas that dominate my thinking, I discard those which limit me. I give greater thought to those which give me control over experiences. By means of right ideas, I operate my consciousness to give me what I want. I do this with joy for I know the results which follow.

MY INTUITION IS MY GUIDE

The Infinite Spirit saturates all creation with Its loving Presence. It is in all and in action at every point in time and space. So, Its beloved action is in my consciousness as direct clear knowing. This is my God-given intuition. It is the inner Mind which knows what I need to know at the instant I need to know it. Right ideas are always waiting in my consciousness for me to use for my good and the good of others.

I now let my intuition guide me in enhancing every area of my life and affairs. I now reject all fear, all worry and all uncertainty. I am free of all negatives. Divine Ideas are the answer to my present problems. My consciousness knows this and welcomes these ideas and gives them the substance of its thought and feeling. These ideas contain all power and all knowing. They proceed to do great things by means of me.

I appreciate the creative ideas which my intuition gives to me today. They direct my consciousness to bring forth the new, the improved and the wholesome ways of living. I follow through on these spiritual ideas in my material affairs. Intuitive ideas maintain me in health, freedom in money and a happy attitude.

3

WISDOM

___

I LIVE WITH WISDOM

I am the embodiment of all the Life there is, for God is all the Life there is. All Mind, Love and Truth are at this instant in full action in my consciousness. I am wise with the wisdom of the Spirit. There is no hesitation in my knowing that God gives to me out of the bounty of Itself all right ideas. These are my resource of all that I need and want. I give them freedom of action in my thinking.

These right ideas are my inner wisdom of being. No more shall ignorance of the Truth misdirect my creative thinking. I now renounce all possibilities of mistakes. Neither past ones nor present ones disturb me. I am rid of them. I proceed with my affirmative living today and in the days that yet shall be. All my thinking is spiritually based, and all my creations are good. They are of value in my living and increase the good in this world.

Living with wisdom, I have nothing to fear. Negatives have no authority in consciousness. I am undisturbed by people, situations and world opinions. I think of the things I want, knowing that they are now manifesting. Life never lets me down. It supports and maintains me in the goodness of everyday living. I praise the Mind of God in action in my thinking right now.

I LIVE WISELY AND I LIVE WELL

Being one with all Mind, I am one with all Wisdom. In my consciousness is this spiritual wisdom. Knowing this, I have good judgment in handling my own thoughts and emotions. I control them in ways of creative directions. I eliminate all anger, all fear and all false imaginations. My inner peace is obvious to me and to others. Other persons' judgments and pronouncements of so-called truth do not disturb my right thinking. My inner wisdom maintains me in poise and in true authority over my own experience.

I discern the ideas that are true and eliminate all false concepts. I am alert to negative ideas, situations and people. I clear my consciousness of these and I truly know the good that is mine. My wisdom expands every form of prospering patterns in my subconscious mind. My good is growing daily in ways of love and ease. I praise the spiritual power of growth which is now in action in every area of my health consciousness. I enjoy my present life with its fullness of ease.

My inner wisdom provides me with ways of growth in loving, in appreciating people and in giving of my best to the busy world of my affairs. I praise the Presence and the Power of God always active in my consciousness. I am anchored in Truth today.

4

CREATIVITY

I AM THE CREATIVE POWER

There is one creative power, the Power of God, the Power of Mind. I am a divinely created individual endowed with the Power to create the new and the better. My consciousness is God's thinking process, and it is all power to its creation. It acts through me with total authority. It dissolves all negatives and expresses through all affirmatives.

My consciousness is spiritually sensitive to right ideas. It rejects all negative possibilities. It harbors no false opinions, and it never sits in judgment. It knows the Truth and creates after the ideas of Truth. Its creations are always beneficial to me and to my fellow man. My spiritual thinking is the guarantee of my health. It maintains my body in right activities. This healthy thinking is also the basis of my prosperity. It releases from my thinking all fear of lack in the present and in the future.

Knowing that what I want does not take from the good of anyone, I create it with wisdom. My own creations maintain me in well-being. They glorify the good which is God. They benefit those with whom I work. I rejoice in the creative power of my spiritual knowing.

TODAY I AM A CREATIVE PERSON

God, the All Mind, created me to do great things and to be a great and loving individual. I now accept myself as this valuable person. The Divine Consciousness never measures me by the past, my errors or my faults. It knows me this day as Its beloved creation with unlimited possibilities. It knows neither age nor handicaps. It expects me to be the finest consciousness and the finest creator of good. In God's thought I am unlimited and unconditioned. This is the Truth of what I really am.

My mind is at peace. There is no resistance to good nor argument with my good. I let the Divine Right Action take over my consciousness and I now create greater creations than I have ever created before. I am inspired by the ideas of the Spirit which are active in my thought. I no longer repeat the past. I fashion the new, the better and the more advanced. Tomorrow's ideas take place in my consciousness today. By means of me, what ought to be will be. I give my full mental attention to the ideas now being born in my consciousness.

The Law of Mind accepts this new thinking of mine and acts upon it. I now rest knowing that my mind has done its creative work and has done it well.

5

LIFE AND HAPPINESS

MY PRESENT LIFE IS GOD'S ACTION

My life is a free, unlimited and unconditioned gift from that Mind which causes all. It is impersonal yet becomes personal as I live it with wisdom. I decide what this Life shall be and do as my life in action. I now select all ideas in my consciousness, to be certain that they make my life as I want it to be. I have health, vitality and freedom of body movements. I like my life.

I do not self-limit my life and the freedom it gives me to do all that I want to do. I am not a complainer, and all subconscious patterns of dissatisfaction and complaining are now erased and gone. With them are erased all disease possibilities. I am the health of life. I am the vitality of life. I am the well-being of life. My body bears witness that this is so. I look alive and vital to all who know me.

I am divinely flexible. There is no rigidity in my consciousness or in my body. Thinking spiritual thoughts keeps me in vibrant health. I affirm the spirituality of my body, and of all the processes in it which maintain me in freedom of action. My healthy thinking has no place for negative ideas. My right knowing of Truth gives them no room in my mind or body. My present life is God's beloved activity.

I LIKE MY PRESENT LIFE

I know that all life is God in action. It is the activity of the One Mind, and that action is my life here and now. All that I am and all that I have is this spiritual activity. I am receptive to all that It is giving to me and revealing through me. My consciousness has in it all the ideas of life in its fullness. These make easy and perfect my way. These are my spiritual life insurance.

There is no room in my thinking for unpleasantness. I have spiritual understanding and I live and work in peace with my fellow man. I find the good in every situation. I like people and they are aware that I like them. My present life is alive with good both known and unexpected. I praise the spiritual basis of my life today. It inspires me to do even greater things and to grow in ways of wisdom.

There is no fear, worry or false concern about negatives and their possible resulting activities. My knowledge of God as my consciousness, which in turn is my life, my affairs and all my relationships, solves every problem as it arises. I am always victorious. As I know and live the Truth, I am never afraid. All that I need I have this day.

NOW IS THE APPOINTED TIME

The Infinite Mind is not governed by a calendar. In my consciousness the Infinite Mind is not divided into the past, the present and the future. I am in that now which is all that God knows and in which all Mind operates. All my thinking is current thinking. I like all I am in present time. I never compare it with the past, nor with dreams of the future. I am a now person in a wonderful now consciousness.

I refuse to be mentally haunted by my mistakes. All time for me is now, and I have cleared my subconscious mind of these. I also refuse to be blinded by false hopes and dreams of future triumphs. My consciousness today is creating future experiences by my right thinking now. All the good I have ever known is still a part of my conscious now. All the good I will ever have is in my consciousness awaiting my unfoldment of its ideas.

I am constantly upheld by the Mind and Heart of God. This is my time to experience all the good which I am and can be. I have no self-rejection. I know I am spiritually worthy of great good now, and I mentally accept this as the truth right where I am now.

LIFE EXPECTS ME TO BE HAPPY

The Life of God created me out of Itself in order to know Itself more completely by means of my consciousness. I am all that the Infinite is or ever shall be. I am a full expression of the Joy of the Spirit. My consciousness accepts this as the Truth of my being, because it is just that. The opposite feelings, which are anti-joy, have no power or authority in me. I reject them and I reject all people and situations which could cause my unhappiness.

There is no spiritual causation to unhappiness. It is falsely created in consciousness. It has no part of the real I AM which I really am. I refuse to lower my thinking to believe in it. All my thinking is affirmative and based on God's Ideas, which are the only true creative sources from which I draw my good. These create in my consciousness and in my everyday living a fullness of Life, Love and Happiness.

I refuse to be depressed by world conditions and by negative friends and family members who are always worrying. I have too much to do that is creative and valuable to listen to their complaints. My consciousness is free of all negative speculation. I am Joy, and Happiness is my way of living this day. For this, I give thanks.

I AM GLAD TO BE ALIVE

The divine Life is rich, full and free. I know I am this Life in total action today. This Life is the movement of divine consciousness through my awareness. I have an alive consciousness with an alive body, and there is new life in all my affairs and all my personal relationships. For me, life is never old nor measured. It is vital and new in every way. Divine Life is in action right now in all my activities, creating expanding good.

God's Life in action in my consciousness does not know illness, age or death. It only knows me as Its beloved action. Therefore, every negative and false belief about life in my subconscious mind is now uprooted and gone. I am free to live joyously. Knowing this, my health is splendid, all my affairs prosper, and I am at ease with all people.

There is a wonder to all life, and I sense its spiritual origin and spiritual continuity. It is amazing what the Life of God in me has done, is doing and will always be doing. Its resources are boundless and all that It is, is mine to be. I am glad to have this knowledge of Life as the Truth.

6

THIS DAY

I APPRECIATE THIS DAY

Mind unlimited is in action in my consciousness today. This Infinite Spirit knows me as Its Creative means of self-expression. I am the inlet and the outlet of all Its Ideas. These alone are the source of my spiritual thinking and creative doing. New Ideas stimulate my thinking, bringing forth right action in all my affairs. I appreciate this.

All power in any negatives in my consciousness is now diffused and gone. Affirmative and loving living is mine in these good hours of possibility. I relax for I am now free of all stress and strain. My consciousness is cleared of all fear. My thinking and feeling is worthy of my divine birth. Right now I have the joy and the peace which comes from my spiritual well-being.

I know myself as a whole person. All that I need for this day I have. All health, prosperity and love are evident in my consciousness. Others are aware of my quickened spiritual thought and feeling. I give sincere affection to my friends and loved ones. I am at peace with myself and everyone else. Tonight I shall sleep with ease and give thanks for this day. It is truly the day of the Lord.

YESTERDAY IS FINISHED

Today is my day for creative right action producing affirmative results greater than any that I have created before. My consciousness is uncluttered by old patterns, old hurts and wrong opinions. In my thinking, Yesterday is finished and gone from my thought. I am free to proceed with the business of fresh living, thinking and feeling. I have every idea I need to do this. In my consciousness the one Mind, God, alerts me to these great spiritual ideas. I know their value and I use them.

With joy I release all outworn ideas from my thinking. The negatives of Yesterday have gone and I am now a new thinker in a better experience. I create my good by knowing in joy that my good is truly mine. All the channels in my consciousness are causing it to happen and it is now a fact. I do not hope, I know. My knowing is causative to my experience. I hold fast to my dream and my expectations of good, and my thinking makes it so. I am changing into a better and finer individual.

I respect the good, the beauty and the love I have known. However, I keep my thinking and feeling fresh and creative in this day and in the great days to come. Such days are God's gift to me.

I LIKE TODAY AND EVERY DAY

Today is alive with possibilities. These twenty-four hours are the action of God revealing to me that which I really am and that which I can be. It is an affirmative day saturated with Life, Intelligence, Love and Beauty. This is the day in which I am encouraged to do greater things than any I have ever done before. It is my day to live fully, to love greatly and to think rightly. My consciousness knows the Truth and works from the premise of Truth right now.

My consciousness functions today with new ideas. The negatives of yesterday have no place in my thinking today. I release all personal judgments of people, situations and governments. I forgive and forget past hurts. I am in this day of fresh thought and fresh feeling. I sustain its spiritual purity. I like this day and during it I expect only the good and the right. My thinking is spiritually premised as I know the Truth and affirm that my consciousness is spiritually sound.

This is my day of demonstration. I relax from all tension and let the action of God take place in all my thought and feeling. I am totally receptive to my highest good and now accept the ideas which will produce it. Today is wonderful. It is the goodness of God where I am.

7

MY GOOD

WHERE I AM MY GOOD IS

I am always in the Presence of the Infinite Mind. That Mind is always in action in my consciousness. Its ideas are my source of instant wisdom and correct knowing. I affirm that these great ideas now operate in all my thinking, feeling and doing. They announce to my consciousness that the Good that I want I already have. I do not need to travel in body or mind. My Good is God in action at this moment in my consciousness. Being of the Spirit, It is free of all conditioning in the world of false ideas. My Good is now, and I subconsciously accept this as the Truth because it is the Truth.

All power acts upon this clear knowing of mine. There is nothing to oppose, limit or delay my good. My good is independent of the process which demonstrates it now. It is divinely authorized by my spiritual acceptance of it. My decision that it is mine causes it to happen. I relax from all worry and other negative speculations. These have no place or influence in my thought.

I contemplate my Good as being factual. It appears in my experience on time and in order and in loving ways. I give thanks to that Mind for causing it to be. I rejoice and am glad that this is the Truth.

I APPRECIATE THE GOOD WHICH IS MINE

God works in my consciousness in wonderful ways. This is the knowing factor in all my thinking. It is the creativity of my consciousness. I appreciate what the Infinite Spirit is doing in me, for me and in all my affairs. I am inspired at every moment of this day. I am aware of a divine purpose and a divine order in my affairs. All things do work together as my good.

I waste no time in worry or negative thinking. I let the God Consciousness give me the idea I need for each piece of work I need to do, and I do it on time and in order. I do not delay my good by procrastinating. Infinite Intelligence is always in action in every thought I have and in all the work I do. Living the spiritual life of God, I am at peace with my activities, and I enjoy all I do. I accomplish with ease and joy.

I appreciate the good which is mine. It is the result of my consciousness and its correct thinking and knowing. It reminds me of the foolishness of worry and strain. These have no place nor function in my consciousness. I am privileged to know I am the Truth and that I lovingly express this Truth.

8

PROBLEMS

—

I AM NOT A PROBLEM PERSON

The Infinite Mind never created a problem and has never known of a problem. I was born of that Mind as a problemless individual. The Mind and Love of the Infinite are my spiritual parents. To me they have given the total wisdom and intelligence of life. All my so-called inheritance was spiritual and contained no problems from the past. Today is my day to be free of any problem or situation that I believe to be mine.

I set myself free of problems by knowing the Truth that they are temporary and have no reality or permanence. There is no place in my consciousness for negative states of worry and fear. All my spiritual energies are geared to the solutions of troubles so that they move out of my life right now. This they do, for I no longer maintain them by thinking and re-thinking them. I am now free to think ahead and create what I really want.

All Mind and Its Ideas give me the new directions I need to be creative and productive. In my consciousness, this action is taking place, and I instantly know what to do and I do it. There is no hesitation in my thought. There is no sense of not being worthy of the greater good I am causing to be. Free of problems, I am valuable to God and to my fellowman.

I AM GREATER THAN MY PROBLEM

All Mind is centered in my consciousness. All ideas I already have. I am fully aware that I alone can solve my problems. I do not lean on other people's human opinions. I know what to do and I do it from the Divine Center in my consciousness. I am a controlled thinker in a controlled situation. Knowing that I am a total spiritual individualization of the One Mind, I have no fear of problems and no doubt about my handling them.

I am equal to every situation that faces me. I affirm that there is no power or reality in any problem. Negatives are now neutralized by this treatment which is the Word of God declared into the Law of Mind. My consciousness is activated by Divine Intelligence, so I always see past the problem to the solution. I know that any problem is a temporary effect of a negative cause. There is no permanence to negatives. They appear in order to disappear. There is no spiritual substance in them.

Divine Wisdom in action in my consciousness at this moment gives me the ideas I need, and I use them to solve my difficulty. This they do, and I am free to move forward to greater things. I praise my inner resources which always support me in my right doing.

I AM WITHOUT FEAR

There is nothing in the Eternal, Causative Mind to create fear. In God it has no truth and no reality. Knowing this, I now set myself free of all beliefs of fear. It is a false impediment that restricts my abilities and disturbs my emotions. I decree in my consciousness that all fear is now annihilated and cannot reappear in my thought. Now I am free to be my total great Self.

The world in which I live is a pleasant one. It invites me to explore it and reap all kinds of good from it. Without fear, I can appreciate it and greatly benefit from its beauty and peace. I do not fear the changing seasons. Each gives of itself to me in different ways. I agree with all forms of weather, and fear neither hot nor cold. I sense the omnipresence of the Living Spirit in all nature and in all people.

Without fear in my consciousness, I now can appreciate all men, women and children. Like myself, they are all spiritual beings on their individual pathways. I cannot be hurt by anyone for there is nothing in my consciousness to create this. All people share love with me, and I share my love with them. Every area of my daily living is greater as a result of my mental freedom.

9

HEALTH

GOD'S HEALTH IS MY HEALTH

The one Life, God, which is perfect and indestructible, created me out of Itself. It created me with definite purpose to express spiritual and physical health for all the years I am around this great world. I accept health as a spiritual gift. I maintain it with wisdom. I keep my thinking healthy and my consciousness in harmony so that all I want to do I am able to do. I refuse to make myself sick with worry and fear.

New creative ideas fill my consciousness with new thinking and planning. These are health to my mind. They are mental food, nourishing ideals and expectancies. They take away stress and strain. They reassure me of all the good that is mine when I accept and praise it. I know I am the Life of God. I know I am worthy of health in all its forms. I am known by others as a healthy individual. I am vitally and joyously alive.

I check my consciousness to be sure it is health-motivated and health-interested. I refuse to let world thought of possible illness ever have entrance to my thinking. I know my health is spiritual and divine and always will be. I give thanks that this is so because it is so.

I PRAISE THE SOURCE OF MY HEALTH

God, as Mind, Love and Truth is in complete action in my consciousness this day. The cause of my health and its continuity is my consciousness. I know that there is no physical or material cause of my health. The perfect circulation of spiritual ideas in my thought is the true source of my well-being. I praise my awareness of this Truth. I am Health. I look like Health. I talk healthily.

New and fresh ideas interest me. I accept them gladly and my consciousness assimilates them. I now let all old and outworn ideas leave my subconscious mind, and they shall not return. I appreciate their value at one time, but I want them no more. Spiritual ideas hold my attention right now and shall continue to do so. These ideas create for me more health, more vitality and more joy.

Knowing that the Divine Mind is the cause of my Health, I expect it to continue fully from this day onward. It shall not be limited by other people's opinions of age, weather, diet or stress. I am an individual thinker in the One Mind and I think health and life independently of all the world warning of illness. I cannot be convinced of anything but the Truth. My consciousness knows its Source and I am healthy-minded.

SPIRITUAL THINKING HEALS

The Divine Spirit in my consciousness is completely able to free me from all that would limit or obstruct my freedom in living fully this day. Its total right knowing is in charge of all my thinking-feeling nature. God's Intelligence illuminates and heals all incorrect thought I may have. It is undaunted by illness in any form. It knows it not. In my consciousness It knows that it cannot be, for I am a spiritual creation and therefore I am perfect.

All erroneous causation in my thinking is now eliminated by the action of Truth which is always correct in its conclusions. It knows me as Its beloved individual through whom It glorifies Itself. Perfect life and health circulate throughout my consciousness. These eliminate all my false speculations of illness and its possible consequences. I again know my Source and its perfect action in me and through me. I am that Health which is God.

My correct spiritual thinking heals me of all that is unlike the Truth. I am now free of all negative possibilities of trouble. The ever-renewing life of the Spirit maintains me in well-being and in effective living. I am able to function well and have peace of mind. I am now secure in living. My consciousness gives me healthy ideas to use for richer living.

I KNOW MY HEALTH IS SPIRITUAL

I know that God is all in all and in action by means of all. Therefore my life and health are spiritual and divine. In my consciousness the ideas of life and health are complete ideas containing within themselves every thought and every lesser idea for their full expression in my outer living. My health is certain and unchanging.

I now decree that my subconscious mind releases and nullifies all negative patterns of disease in any of its obnoxious forms. I am not medical symptoms. I am spirit and I am life. I am health with all its enthusiasm and vitality for full and happy living. My spiritual health maintains me in freedom of body to do all the things which I want to do, and to do them with ease.

Healthy ideas fill full my consciousness. There is no place in my thinking for fear of illness. I live in healthy ways. I use spiritual ideas of wisdom regarding the care of my body. I appreciate and praise my health for it is God's Life in my consciousness. I think rightly about myself and the functions of my world.

I talk health. I affirm this health for the people who are close to me. I know that spiritual health belongs to everyone. I subconsciously accept this treatment. I exhibit my consciousness of health.

MY THOUGHT MAINTAINS MY HEALTH

My health is spiritual in essence and perfect in its manifestation. It gives me total ease in my operation of life. God, the living Spirit almighty, is the source and continuity of my physical well-being. My consciousness knows this and my right thinking about my health maintains it in fullness. I make certain that my thinking is based on creative and worthy ideas. These ideas are already in my consciousness awaiting my use of them.

I expect to be healthy this day and every day. I discipline my habits of everyday living to be sure of this God-given health. I refuse to indulge in worry, fear or hurts. These are disease-prone and have no place in my thought and feeling nature. They are not of God and they cannot limit my health. The Divine Mind does not know negatives, and I am born of that Mind. I think health, appreciate my health and praise my health. All the energies of my mind and body are working in complete accord, creating and maintaining my health.

My health is free of the false belief of age, inheritance and weather. Health is spiritual and divine. Knowing this, I am not subject to other persons' opinions about my health. My health consciousness is spiritually maintained by my right thinking.

I ENJOY MY HEALTH

All life includes the ability to have pleasure, because all life is Divine in origin and in daily action. I know this and enjoy as much of life as I can grasp and experience. I value my knowledge of God, the One Mind, as the creator of all that I am and all that I shall ever be. My health is from that Source, and I do those things which will sustain it in fullness.

My thinking is healthy, for my consciousness is healthy. All subconscious mental and emotional patterns which could cause discomfort and illness are now erased by this treatment which is the Word of God spoken into the Law of Mind. This Word which I declare is all power and executes itself. Right ideas maintain my consciousness in healthy attitudes. Today's fresh thinking reveals the ever new life that I have.

Living in health and well-being, I do not expect illness in any form. My health is spiritual and complete. I know this and I speak this as the Truth of my being. I cancel all negative thinking as soon as it appears in my consciousness. It finds no dwelling place in my thought. Today I am healthy, happy and feel wonderful. I praise the health of God which is mine now and evermore shall be.

10

WEALTH

I PRAISE MY WEALTH IN GOD

All that I am and all that I have is the result of divine causation. I am the embodiment of the living Spirit. I am God in action this day. I give thanks that in the divine order my wealth is established, in action in my consciousness. It inspires me to live wisely. I accept my prosperity as being right and ever expanding in my consciousness. Every idea I need to maintain and increase the flow of prosperity is now in my thought, and I use it for my good.

My good never lessens, because spiritual causation never retreats. Former patterns of worry or fear regarding money are eliminated from my subconscious mind by this treatment which is the word of Truth spoken into the Law of Mind. Every door which needs to be opened for the continuous flow of money into my activities is now open.

All I need financially is established in my consciousness before I need it. My prosperity, being spiritually based, is not influenced by worldly opinions and other people's advice. As a spiritual individual I am independent in clear thinking. I give thanks that I know God is my source and that I shall always have all that I need whenever I need it.

MY RESOURCES ARE INEXHAUSTIBLE

All that the Eternal Mind and Goodness has is mine to use in right and loving ways for my own happiness and the happiness of those I love. There are no restrictions in the spiritual giving of Life Itself to me. I am able to have all that I want in each day of my living now. The Bounty awaits my recognition. It has no favorite people to whom It gives. I am a spiritual being worthy of the fullness of being. I know the generosity of the Spirit. It takes care of all my needs and desires when I know It is doing so.

I cannot afford poverty thinking with its subtle ways of making me feel that I cannot afford the best there is. All such negative patterns in my subconscious mind are now uprooted and gone by this treatment which is the Word of Truth declared in the Law of Mind. I am now free to draw upon my inexhaustible spiritual resources and to really feel at ease in my prospering living.

I give thanks for the ever-flowing and increasing good in my life. I appreciate the Mind and Heart of Being for my life well lived and the love I give and receive daily. I know that all is well in my consciousness.

I LET PROSPERITY HAPPEN

In the allness of God, I eternally dwell. Infinite Mind is my consciousness and right ideas are always in action in this consciousness. I know that all that I want is being given to me right now by that Spirit which is God. My prosperity is, and now I let it happen.

Any and all negative patterns in my subconscious mind regarding money, finances and the supposed virtue of poverty are now erased. They are released from my thought. They can never again influence my thinking. My prosperity is an actual fact in my experience this day. Whatever needs to be done to reveal its presence is done in right action and right ways by God, the living Spirit almighty.

It is mine and I know it. I think in its terms. I act in prosperous ways. I now have no fear of future financial needs or strains. The Divine Abundance is mine by right of consciousness and can never leave me. I rejoice and give thanks that this is so. I appreciate the perfect ideas of plenty now functioning in my consciousness.

My faith is in the prospering ideas of the Spirit. These enrich my thinking and maintain me in right knowing. They remove all doubt and negative speculation. I know the Truth of my Prosperity, and my whole consciousness accepts it fully and acts upon this new premise with joy.

I EXPECT THE GREATEST

All Life is mine to use for the expansion of goodness in my experience. The Infinite Mind cannot by Its very nature withhold any ideas from my consciousness. I am the means by which the Infinite creates on the level of the finite. I am total Mind in action at this moment and throughout this day. All the ideas I need now or at any time in the future are in my consciousness right now.

Knowing this clearly, I let my prosperity happen. I mentally accept this as a completed and fulfilled idea in my consciousness. Any and all subconscious patterns which are contrary to this Truth are now erased and gone from my thought. All that I need to prosper in every area of my life is now in action in my consciousness, and I give this omnipotent creative flow my complete cooperation. I expect the greatest that can be to now take place in my affairs.

I am prosperity. I think prosperity. I love prosperity. I have no condemnation of money or others' use of it. My money is spiritual in cause and wonderful in effect. I use it with wisdom. I appreciate all its benefits. It is a constant evidence of the glory of God giving me security and peace of mind. I am enriched by the Truth of my being.

I AM SUPPORTED BY LIFE

My prosperity is a portion of Universal Supply which is God in action. It is permanent in my consciousness, offering the fullness of life. This inner resource is independent of my age, of self-imposed limitations to my abundant good. It is always available when I think spiritually and affirm I am supplied by an unrestricted Mind.

I now accept my freedom in money. I respect money, for I know it is a spiritual idea to maintain me in ease of action. It cannot withhold itself. It has no mind of its own. My consciousness is the deciding factor, and I have decided I have, will always have money in its varying forms, supporting all I want to be and do. It always happens in my affairs in right ways through right channels.

I use money with wisdom, but I am never self-stingy. I am generous with others and pay my bills on time. I have no envy of others' wealth. I have this inner spiritual resource which supplies my way of life completely. Affirmative thinking maintains me in freedom of finance. I appreciate divine supply in my affairs. I give thanks to the Mind and Heart of God which created me and is maintaining me.

The author wishes to thank Arthur Vergara
and DeVorss & Company
for their splendid cooperation.

R. C. B.

Subconscious mind in me. you knew
it, so do it.